GOD,
—MONEY—
& YOU

GOD, MONEY & YOU

101 Spiritual Answers To Your Financial Questions

PHILIP L. LIBERATORE
CPA, IRS Problem Solver & Ordained Minister

dlm
PUBLISHING
La Mirada, CA

Table of Contents

Acknowledgements

GOD HAS ENRICHED MY LIFE with so many wonderful relationships. These people have been God's love and faithfulness extended to me and I want to take this opportunity to acknowledge them as a tremendous source of encouragement and strength:

I am eternally grateful to my precious wife, Dana. She has faithfully and selflessly given her love and support to champion me to become all that I can be in every area of my life. Our Lord has truly blessed me with an amazing wife, whom I love very much. Our life verse is Proverbs 3:5-6: "Trust in the Lord with all your heart and lean not on your own understanding; in all your ways acknowledge Him, and He will direct your path." I am truly blessed that God has directed our paths to be joined together.

My overwhelming and abounding appreciation for my precious daughters, Lisa and Marci, who are the loves of my life and who have a wonderful way of keeping me young! Being their Dad has been one of the greatest privileges and joys of my life.

My wonderful parents, Mario and Celeste, who have always encouraged me to pursue personal and professional excellence.

My pastors: Dr. Paul Risser, who instilled the Biblical principles of stewardship and giving into my life through his teachings, example, and personal counsel, and to Rev. Terry Risser, whose friendship and pastoral care have been priceless to me.

My brothers in Christ: Sam, Bob, and Hector, who meet with me every Friday morning for fellowship, prayer, Bible study, and accountability. These men have been an anchor of support to me.

My pal Adam Christing, who is always an inspiration to me and who was instrumental in coordinating the publishing of this book. His positive influence in my life is truly a gift.

My committed staff on which I depend daily. I value and appreciate their dedication to excellence in partnering with me, as we serve our clients together.

Introduction

Your money matters to God.

YOU MAY BE ASKING, "Why does my money matter to God?" I am convinced that money plays a key role in your spiritual development. The way you manage your money is linked to your heart transformation.

This paradigm shift will revolutionize the way you give, and most importantly, the way you live. You will be part of the excitement of advancing the Kingdom of God. This is the heart of the matter: Giving to God and being others-focused. Too many times when it comes to money we are self-focused, looking for what we can get rather than how the process of being God's "steward" can help conform us to the image of Christ.

I would like to share my personal story with you. God has weaved His money-management principles into the fabric of my life. There was a season in my life when I was without a job. I had no income. I exhausted all of my options trying to get employment. I sent out approximately 600 resumes.

I was in a difficult position. Each day I was being forced to take from my depleting savings. My ability to trust God was definitely being stretched. But in seeking God's direction and searching out His Word, the Lord led me to Malachi 3:10: "Bring the whole tithe into the storehouse, that there may be food in my house. Test me in this," says the Lord Almighty, "and see if I will not throw open the floodgates of heaven and pour out so much blessing that you will not have room enough for it."

As I read these words, the Holy Spirit began to transform my heart. Did I read this right; the Lord Almighty was asking me to test Him in the area of my money? You got it! There was absolutely no way that I was going to withhold my tithe from the Lord, even though I had absolutely no income. I continued to be faithful to God and continued tithing to the church 10% of what my prior income had been.

I continued giving like this for seven months. God miraculously provided for my needs. It was after those long seven months that God led me to a tax attorney who helped me establish my own tax business. This was the beginning of a journey in which God has continued to show himself miraculous in many ways. From the truth of Malachi 3:10 and from this excruciating, yet transforming experience, God put me on a journey that has turned out to be a dream of a lifetime. In my experience, this biblical priority of giving to God first is the cornerstone principle regarding money.

Through the years, God has taken His words and has embedded them deeper into my heart. He continues to show me the power of consecrated giving. Every year from that time forward, I have put God to the test, as he invites in Malachi 3:10. What an incredible experience. God is faithful and true. I can guarantee you this: You can never out-give God. I challenge you to give beyond your comfort level.

Some years I have tithed based on the income I wanted to

make. You read that right. My giving was based on income I wanted to make, not the income I was generating at the time. God blessed me. A few years later, I was making that larger income I had tithed on. Recently, I have given the Lord one tenth of what I wanted to make for the year upfront—right in the beginning of January.

It has been incredible. God has given back to me time and time again so that I can financially support numerous ministries and outreach organizations. God is incredible! What an amazing opportunity we have to partner with Him. It's true, your money matters to God. When you start giving and managing your money God's way, He will transform your life and your ability to give to others. God will bless you.

He wants to raise your standard of giving.

This book will help you. It is filled with valuable insights and financial information, all from a God-glorifying perspective. These principles have been proven in my life and in the lives of my tax and accounting clients. These 101 Spiritual Answers to Your Financial Questions are time-tested and life-tested.

You may be currently hurting over money issues. Every day I speak with people who are in pain because of financial losses, economic struggles, and the relationship difficulties that often surround money. Many people find themselves wishing they could win the lottery, thinking their money problems would go away. In reality, most of our problems have little to do with money itself. Your relationship with money can be a great source of bitterness. But if you put God first, it can be a real source of blessing. It depends on you.

This book can help you rid yourself of bad money habits so that you can develop new ones that will work for you. I wrote this book to help you develop a healthy, God-honoring perspective about money so you can be free to enjoy the important people in your life.

The best answers to your toughest questions about money can't be found in the tax code. They are found in the Good Book. Along with Scriptural principles, I have provided you with many practical suggestions for dealing with your money and your life. When you change your mindset about money, you can experience a brighter financial future.

I am a CPA and an "IRS Problem Solver." In my line of work, I have seen people literally set free from financial bondage. I love what I do. It is God's truth that sets us free. Over the years, God has revealed to me explicit, life-changing principles about money that I would like to share with you.

I invite you to take the concepts in *God, Money & You* and incorporate them into your heart and life. It is my prayer that you will experience all that God has in store for you.

If you find you are in need of professional services, I would love to hear from you. My contact information is located at the back of the book.

God bless you.

Phil Liberatore
La Mirada, California

GOD AND MONEY

"Seek first the Kingdom of God."

—MATTHEW 6:33

1 **Isn't money the root of all evil?**

No. That's become a famous saying, but it's not actually what the Bible states. The actual text from 1 Timothy 6:10 reads: "For the love of money is at the root of all kinds of evil. Some people, craving money, have wandered from the faith and pierced themselves with many griefs."

Money, in and of itself, cannot be evil. It's an inanimate object! You'll never hear about a dollar bill robbing a bank. Checkbooks don't steal…it's people who can steal your checkbook. Evil is in people, not in money. It's just that money (and power, and fame, and pride, and…) can and often does bring out the worst in us.

So what the Apostle Paul is warning about is lusting after money. Contrary to that famous scene in the movie *Wall Street*, greed is not good. Paul goes on to warn his young disciple, Timothy, that some people have abandoned their faith by craving money and going after it with reckless abandon. That can ruin your life.

Money can, and often does, bring out the worst in us.

So here's the bottom line about the bottom line: Money is a neutral or even good thing. But be warned: Lusting after money for money's sake will lead to all sorts of evil in your life. Don't let it happen to you. Put God first.

2 What does the Bible say about money?

A whole bunch! Did you know that in the New Living Translation of the Bible, the word "money" is used 84 times? The word "hymn" is only used two times. God is definitely concerned about our attitude towards money. More specifically, He cares about your involvement with money. It matters to God:

- *How you earn it*

- *That you save it*

- *If you are willing to share it*

- *And much, much more*

The Bible doesn't just say one thing about money; it says hundreds of things about it. God blesses people financially (remember the story of Abraham when God promised to bless him and his descendants?). God also gives warnings to rich people who make money or their appetites their "god." See the book of James chapter one for several examples.

Jesus' commandment to "Seek first the Kingdom of God, and all these things shall be added to you," (Matthew 6:33) may be the best concise summary of God's perspective on all of your needs. Put Him first and He'll take care of the rest...including your money matters.

3 Does God want me to have money?

Yes. But He is more concerned about your heart than He is about your bank account. God's main desire for you is that you put your trust in Him (not in money, your spouse, your job, or your own strength).

God does bless people financially. In fact, God is so good, "the rain falls on the just and the unjust." (Matthew 5:45) But He especially loves to give gifts to His children. If you have kids or grandkids, aren't you the same way? And along those lines, would you keep giving your kids gifts if they weren't grateful, didn't take care of them, or didn't share them? You'd discipline them in love so that they would learn to appreciate and share the good things you give them.

> *God is more concerned about your heart than your bank account.*

God is the same way. He doesn't need your money. He owns everything. He wants to see you dependent on Him, the source of every good gift.

Christians differ in thought about how God wants His children to prosper. My reading of the Scripture teaches me that God, indeed, wants to pour out a blessing on His children… That means you. He wants you to be a good "steward" or manager of what He shares with you. If He can trust you with little, he can trust you with much.

**If the world is going to end,
why should I save money or
make long-term plans?**

Because Jesus told us to be busy about His business and leave the
rest in His hands.

God has not called you to "pin the tail on the antichrist." He
has called you to be faithful to Him. So get to work. We don't
know if planet Earth will be here a few more days or hundreds
and hundreds of years.

Be careful about speculating about the "last days." For some
people, it's a handy excuse for them to not be faithful to the assign-
ment God has given them to glorify Him. You might say, "Why
polish brass on a sinking ship?" But Jesus said, "The gates of hell
will not prevail against my church." So let's get going. Make a
difference. Give money. Make money. Save money.

Plan to live until you are 100. But be ready to go to your real
home tonight!

**Why should I be so concerned
about money, money, money?**

Because Jesus said, "Wherever your treasure is,
there will your heart be also." (Matthew 6:21)

It's not the money itself that is important. It wouldn't matter if people were exchanging seashells, feathers, or rocks. What
matters to God is how we honor Him and how we love others.

Jesus, Himself, made more statements concerning money
than He did about anything else. Never allow money to rule
your life. But at the same time, make sure you observe God's
principles regarding money.

Does God want me to be rich?
You already are in several ways!

- *Your standard of living is already greater than any other generation that has ever lived on planet Earth.*

- *God has blessed you with every spiritual blessing in Christ. If you are a believer, you are "in" Christ. This means that because you are part of God's family, you will inherit Christ's kingdom with Him. Talk about riches!*

If you want to know whether God has promised that you will be a millionaire or a billionaire, I don't think so. BUT God has given you Biblical principles for building and sharing riches. You've been reading about them. He gives to you so that you can give to others.

Give A Lot
Make A Lot
Save A Lot

God will provide enough for you to fulfill your calling.

MONEY AND YOU

*"Money makes a wonderful servant,
but a terrible master."*

—P.T. BARNUM

7 What should my attitude toward money be?

Money is important. But it is not all-important. And if you are poor, don't you dare fall into the trap of thinking that if you were rich you wouldn't have to worry about money. Many poor people idolize money more than the rich do. And, on the flip side, if you have wealth, don't buy into the mistaken idea that if you had less you'd worry about it less.

Jesus says, "Do not worry." (Matthew 6:25) That means that worrying about money (or anything else) is a sin. Let me repeat that: Worrying about money is a sin. Why is that so? Because you can't worry about something and have faith at the same time. And the Bible says, "Whatever is not of faith is of sin."

So then, put on an attitude of gratitude for what you have. That's called contentment. And give thanks to God for what He has already blessed you with and what He will bless you with in the future. Praise God from whom all blessings flow.

8 What does it mean to be a good "manager" of money?

Well, right off the bat, think about that word "manager." In many cases, the manager is not the owner. That's the situation here. It's God's money. In fact, everything belongs

6

to God. (Psalm 24:1) He has given you the role of manager. And it's an important role.

Have you ever been house-sitting for a friend or neighbor? It's a pretty good deal. You get the use of their nice house for a week or so. But if you are a good house-sitter, you like to do a few nice things while the owner has given you the use of the house. You might do some extra watering, some gardening, do a few dishes, take care of a repair—you know what I mean.

Jesus tells us to "occupy until I come." (Notice He didn't say, "Be preoccupied with when I'll come.") We don't know the day that the owner will return. But we want to have His house in order. So here are some more practical ideas:

- *Remember that God is the owner of your money.*

- *Act like it! Take good care of what He has entrusted to you.*

- *Honor Him when He returns, with the way you have taken care of His money through giving, investing, and blessing others with what He has freely shared with you.*

9 Is it wrong for me to accept welfare or other aid?

No, it's not. This book talks a lot about giving to those in need. It's also OK to be on the receiving end when you are in need. In fact, God is glorified when we receive and give thanks. Jesus said that our Father in Heaven loves to give us gifts. Understand something here: Those gifts may come from and through other people.

As far as government programs, you paid into them, so it's OK to get paid from them. Just be careful about not catching the attitude of "working the system" that some have adopted. It amazes me how creative and hard-working some people can be when it comes to getting payouts from the government. If they thought and worked that hard at a job, imagine how successful they could be.

God's Word commands us to bear one another's burdens. But it also says, "If a man will not work, he shall not eat." (2 Thessalonians 3:10) There's an old Jewish saying that some people need to hear at times: "If you are looking for a helping hand, there's one at the end of your arm."

> *It's OK to be on the receiving end when you are in need!*

However, if you are hurting, it is a good thing to receive the gifts, ministering help, and support of others. Be sure to give thanks to God.

10 Is gambling a sin?

My bet is that it is. Sorry, I couldn't avoid that pun. Good Christians differ in opinion on this one, too. I love what Steve Allen once wrote, "I used to make mental bets. That's how I lost my mind."

The only places where the Bible talks about gambling are historical incidents, for example, when the Roman soldiers gambled for Jesus' clothing. But there are biblical principles to remember here:

- *Your life is not your own; it belongs to the Lord. This means that your money belongs to God. Gambling certainly does not provide a good return on God's money.*

- *Gambling has become an epidemic addiction in our culture. The TV shows and movies glorify it, but what they don't show you is the ruined lives, destroyed marriages, crushed hopes, and criminal records that so often accompany the gambling lifestyle.*

- *Set a Godly example for others. Be careful about what you are modeling. The world is watching.*

- *The Bible says, "Whatever is not from faith is sin." (Romans 14:23) So if your conscience bothers you when it comes to the idea of gambling, don't do it!*

By the way, who said that poker was a sport? If you have a gambling problem, get help.

Visit **www.GamblersAnonymous.org.**

 Is it a good idea to borrow money?

Not if you can help it. As the saying goes, "Borrow today, sorrow tomorrow."

You've heard that old expression, "Neither a borrower, nor a lender be." That's incorrect. You want to be a lender. On a personal level, God commands us to give to those in need. (Tip: When you are giving on this level, do so from your giving budget and do not expect a payback.) On an investment level, when you buy mutual funds or invest in the stock market, you are lending. And if you invest wisely, you will usually get a good return.

These are good rules. But of course, there are exceptions.

Keep the following in mind:

- *Don't borrow more than you need.*

- *Try to avoid using credit cards when you borrow. The rates are worse than loan shark rates (avoid loan sharks, too).*

- *Borrow in emergencies if you must.*

- *Borrow when you can use the money wisely with a clear-cut vision for growing the funds. For example, we borrow when we take out a home loan (but isn't it interesting that the original meaning of the root word "mort" in mortgage is death!)*

12 Should I lend money to family or friends?

Yes. In fact, you are commanded to be generous to those in need. (Matthew 5:42)

But, as I mentioned earlier, do not expect to be paid back. Kiss the money goodbye in your heart. Expectations are planned disappointments.

And use funds, if you have them, from your giving budget for this. Do not take from your savings or from your family budget.

Of course, many people say that you should never lend money to family or friends. Why do they say that? Because borrowing and lending can certainly strain relationships. That's why I believe it's best to not expect to get paid back. Don't tell the borrower that, but tell yourself that. It will be good for the borrower to pay you back and that money will go right back into your giving budget. And you can bless someone else with it. A word of caution— think very wisely about giving to friends or family members that have unhealthy money-spending behaviors; be willing to lovingly say no to giving them money: Help them in other ways, and direct them to places of intervention, debtors-anonymous.com, etc.

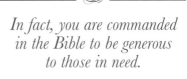

In fact, you are commanded in the Bible to be generous to those in need.

13 What are the biggest mistakes people make with money?

In my 30+ years of experience as a CPA and an IRS Problem Solver, here is my top 10 list of most common mistakes people make with money. They are in no particular order:

- *People have no idea how much money they actually make or how much they are spending.*

- *Most folks have no budget.*

- *Most men and women do not give. They do not abide by God's law of sowing and reaping. Americans spend more on dog food each year than we do on giving to worthy causes!*

- *The majority of people have no financial plan in writing.*

- *Too many people get in trouble with their tax situation or are paying too much in taxes.*

- *Most people are not maximizing their ability to earn money. They are focused on what they can get from work instead of what they can contribute. You'll make more when you contribute more value.*

- *Debt, debt, debt. It's sad, but millions of us are robbing from our futures to pay for our past.*

- *No savings.*

- *Buying the wrong things, and worse, the wrong ideas. You know, ideas have consequences. When you buy into "materialism," for example (and we sure have), you end up with quick thrills, big bills, and your soul not filled.*

- *Fear of success. You read that right. Sure, we fear failure. But many people are afraid to take the chance of living their dreams.*

14   What are the three biggest money wasters?

OK, but it's going to be hard to just name three. I'll give it my best shot:

- *Do you waste money using credit cards and not paying off the balance each month? Right there you are throwing hundreds, maybe thousands of dollars away with those giant monthly interest payments.*

- *Do you buy new at top dollar when you could buy used or generic for far less? This category can cover everything from new cars to vitamins.*

- *Do you pour money into liabilities or assets? Most people waste money on things that are liabilities. Author Robert Kiyosaki says, "A liability eats you, an asset feeds you." Things like new furniture, DVDs, unplanned vacations, impulse shopping – these things eat you. They don't last and they give you no return on your money.*

These are general categories. The specific wasters are numberless. Maybe you spend too much on music, or coffee, or new clothes. Take a hard look at each category and your spending habits. Look for ways to spend more! That's right, you read that right. Spend more on the right things, i.e., giving, serving, marketing your business, your kid's education, your church, your savings and investments.

15 Should I change everything I am doing financially?

No. I see this happen too often.

First off, don't change the things that are working. If you have a good job, a good savings plan, a habit of giving, those are good things. Increase those things.

For problems, change one thing at a time in your financial life.

Where should you start? Well, you can begin by answering this question and taking action on it: What *one* change could you make that would give you and your family the best immediate return? For example:

- *Start something new, like giving to your church, opening an IRA account, or sending a "thank you" to your customers.*

• *Stop something that is hurting you, like giving up drinking (with God's help), saying goodbye to gambling, or not eating out every day for lunch.*

You will feel overwhelmed if you try to make too many changes too soon. Choose the one or two that will give you (and those around you) the biggest lift. Commit to those changes and see the difference in your life.

16 How can I avoid lawsuits?

The Scripture is very helpful here. It says, "Do all that you can to live in peace with everyone." (Romans 12:18)

So don't upset people. If you are in business, under-promise and over-deliver. If you are in a marriage, make it work. Ask God to help you fix the relationship. "Family Law" attorneys get paid when families fall apart.

If someone is threatening to sue you, listen to him or her. Let them blow off some steam. Many times, they just want to be heard. If you have wronged them, make it right.

If you are being attacked in court, you must go on the offensive; even the Apostle Paul defended his rights in court as a Roman citizen. Look out for your family, business, and reputation.

17 Is it OK to take someone to court?

If your issue is with a fellow believer in Christ, you should avoid suing. The New Testament is very clear about this. First, since you share the same Lord, you can work it out. Second, you need to be a good witness to the unbelieving world.

So how can you resolve issues with another believer? Check out Matthew 18:15-17, in which Jesus instructs us about dealing with conflict:

- *Go to your brother or sister privately and directly.*

- *If they won't listen to you, take another believer along with you.*

- *If they still won't listen, take it to the church, i.e., the Elders or church leadership.*

If the person still won't listen, seek counsel which might ultimately lead to court, but this should not be your goal. Try prayer. Try mediation. Try arbitration. Do all that you can to avoid court.

I believe the same principles are true for dealing with non-believers. But we need to be especially on the lookout when it comes to our brothers and sisters in Christ. So, if you have a dispute with a nonbeliever, try to settle it directly, and then through a mediator; finally try legal arbitration. If none of these things is effective, a legal suit may be your only recourse.

18 How can I avoid a costly divorce?

Take that word "divorce" out of your vocabulary, for starters. In certain circumstances, e.g., adultery, you are on biblical grounds for divorce. But even then, God has forgiven you; can you ask Him to help you forgive your spouse? Note: Do not live with or tolerate abuse or allow your children to be abused in any way. Report it and stop it immediately.

Here are some other ways you can "divorce-proof" your marriage:

- *Put God first and your spouse second in all things. (Even before your kids. The best way you can love them is by modeling a successful marriage.)*

- *Never become emotionally or physically intimate with someone of the opposite sex apart from your husband or wife.*

- *Have a regular "just us" time, date night, and getaway weekends.*

- *Do not separate from each other except for times of prayer and fasting.*

If, God forbid, you find yourself in a divorce situation, try to de-escalate the drama. Those arguments and exchanges help nobody but the lawyers who are billing you and your "ex" on an hourly basis. Try to settle things through a mediator, and keep your heart open to reconciliation.

19 I am having trouble making ends meet. What should I do?

My answer might shock you.

Stop focusing on money or your lack of it. Get very focused on what you do best when it comes to work. Get good rest and get to work! Ask your friends, family, and church body to help lift you up emotionally and help take care of your family temporarily, if necessary.

You have to take care of your health and well-being. Cut out every negative influence in your life as much as you can. Stop watching TV. Don't hang around complainers. Do all that you can to create income and ask your creditors to give you extra time to pay them. If possible, create a payback plan that you can live with.

Probably the greatest mistake that people make is to stop tithing in times of financial problems. I have spoken to countless people, who naturally think that this is an area that can be cut. There is nothing further from the truth. It is during these times that God desires to grow our faith and dependence on Him. During these times we have the opportunity to experience the truth of God's principles, first hand. First things first. Be certain that you continue to give God the first fruits of your labor.

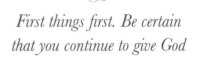

First things first. Be certain that you continue to give God the first fruits of your labor.

DEBT

"You can't put your VISA bill on your
American Express card."

—P.J. O'ROURKE

20 | What is money?

There are as many definitions as there are people.
Here's how I like to think of it: Money is what you
get in exchange for what you give.

This is a helpful definition because it puts the focus on what
you can do to bring value to others. Earl Nightingale once said,
"We get rich by enriching others."

Take the mystery out of money in your life (or the lack of
money). You will have more when you serve more. One of the
economic principles the Western world is founded on is the law
of supply and demand. But this
might be more accurately put:
demand and supply.

> *Money is what you get in*
> *exchange for what you give.*

Money is what is given to
you for supplying what other
people demand (want or need). If what you have to offer is in
high demand, your income will be high. If you increase your
value, you will increase your income.

21 | How can I deal with a money crisis?

My first response might sound harsh. But I'm
going to say it anyway. The best way is to not get
into a money problem to begin with.

But if you're in one and you are feeling hopeless, here's what I suggest:

- *Give your problems to the One who can truly solve them, your Lord and Savior.*

- *Stop doing what you're doing and try a new approach. If you keep doing what you've been doing, you'll keep getting what you've been getting. Do at least one thing differently.*

Make a massive effort to do a "double and divide." This means try to double the amount of work you do (not necessarily the hours, but the results you provide for others). For example, if you are a salesperson and you make 20 outbound calls a day, start making 40. Also, take your expenses and divide them right in half. One half is the "would like to." The other half is the "have to." Pay the "have to" items and hold off on all of the "would like to" items.

22 How can I get out of debt?

The most important thing is to STOP adding to your debt. A word to the wise, "When you're in a hole...stop digging!"

Follow the specific advice outlined in this book. And here's another way to take a stab at it. Have somebody else handle your finances. That's right. Give your checkbook, all but one of your credit cards, and all of your bills to a bookkeeper. This might sound crazy at first. But take a look at that word "accountant." It's where we get the word "accountable" from.

> *When you're in the hole, stop digging!*

You will likely find that you will spend less, save more, and watch your budget better when a professional is handling it with you. Important: You're still in charge, and you need to meet with this person on a regular basis. But now it's not so easy to write a check or hit the ATM every time you feel the urge.

Create a step-by-step get-out-of-debt plan with your CPA, credit counselor, or bookkeeper. Be optimistic, but be realistic. It probably took you 10 to 15 years or more to pile on that debt. How about a three-year plan that you are accountable for following and will have you debt-free except for your house and car? It can be done. And you are more likely to do it if you have a financial professional holding you to it. Key: No more borrowing!

23 Is being in debt wrong or a sin?

Yes. God's Word says, "Owe nothing to anyone except to love one another." (Romans 13:8) Now, please remember a couple of things here:

- *God has a perfect standard and we are not perfect.*

- *God forgives, and if you have put your trust in His Son, He has already forgiven you.*

Also, in our culture, which is a credit-based culture, there are certain things like home ownership that make a lot of sense to buy on credit. This is because, generally speaking, your house will appreciate in value at a greater rate than you will pay in interest on your loan.

Some Christians would say that you should never go into debt for any reason, ever. I think that although that is the best rule of thumb, there are some legitimate exceptions. Home ownership is one. Family or medical emergencies are another.

Please keep in mind that our ultimate debt, the price we deserve to pay because of sin, has been paid in full. We were spiritually bankrupt, but Jesus has released us from our debt. Thank God.

24 Should I cut up all of my credit cards?

I think so! Grab those scissors.

But in our world today, you may really need one credit card for emergencies, as a form of ID, and as a convenience when you don't have a checkbook with you.

Here is a helpful action step. Cut up all of your credit cards except for the following:

- *You don't really need the "Silver" or "Platinum" card, etc. You may find that the benefits are not worth the extra money. Why do I recommend an Amex card? Because you, for the most part, have to pay it off at the end of each month. Plus, there's no interest on the basic green card. Note: Avoid their Optima card. It is just like other high-interest credit cards.*

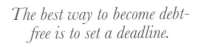

The best way to become debt-free is to set a deadline.

- *A bank ATM/check debit card. These now come with a*

VISA or MasterCard logo on them so you can use them for purchases. But the helpful thing is that the money is taken right from your checking account. That might not feel nice at the moment, but it sure beats the credit card trap of high interest rates and the pain of debt.

25 How soon can I be debt free?

Here's my best guess: On February 28th. Just kidding. But I'm not entirely kidding.

You see, the best predictor of when you'll be out of debt is your own prediction. So set a goal. Have you noticed that when you work on a deadline, a deadline works on you? It's true.

So set an optimistic, but realistic, goal for your debt-free date with destiny. If your debt load is over $10,000, you might have a two-year time frame. It all depends on your income level and necessary expenses.

You can buy computer programs that will take all of your debt data, along with your debt repayment schedule, and spit out an exact time frame you can count on if you stay on schedule.

Personal word: If you get behind, don't get down on yourself. Keep your head up and keep after it. You didn't get into debt overnight. Give yourself time (and the grace) to get out. You can do it. "Let no debt remain outstanding...except the continuing debt to love one another." (Romans 13:8)

26 What tools can help me fix my finances?

Try these five fixers:

- *Put God first and prioritize your giving!*

- *Keep a written record of every dollar that comes in and goes out.*

- *Stick with a budget that covers income, spending, saving, and debt reduction.*

- *Set aside a significant portion of your income for debt elimination, but don't pay down your debt so fast that you can't cover your basic living expenses. Create a specific debt repayment plan.*

- *Pay cash and stop borrowing. Remember: Loans create an insecure future.*

AT WORK

"I used to work in a fire hydrant factory. You couldn't park anywhere near the place."

—STEVEN WRIGHT

27 How can I get a raise?

First, I want to answer this question on a personal level. "When you praise, you get a raise!" This means that your attitude truly does determine your altitude in life. Try it: Praise God and see if you can be depressed at the same time. It's impossible. But I think you are asking me about a financial raise, so here are some tips:

- *Raise your level of commitment and service to your employer.*

- *Raise your number of hours you are working.*

- *Raise the level of responsibility. Become a go-to team player.*

- *Raise your level of expertise. When was the last time you attended a training course or developed a new skill?*

- *Raise the value you bring to your company.*

Finally, *ask* for a raise. But do so in the context of your contribution. Don't say, "Hey, can I have a raise?" Instead say, "Boss, I am so glad to work here. I want you to know that I am making a real effort to help you grow this company. In the last six months, I have improved our computer systems, increased our sales by X amount of money, and I saved us a bunch of money. I estimate that I have earned or saved our company

X amount this year. With this in mind, I am asking for a X amount increase in my annual salary."

Your employer will respect you for asking when you connect your request to your contribution.

28 Should I work more hours?

I think so. There's a lot of talk these days about "working smarter, not harder." Who says you can't do both? God worked six days and rested one. We tend to work four and a half days and goof off for two and a half.

Do I think you should cut into quality time with your husband or wife or kids? No. But TV time is not usually quality time.

What if you went to bed 30 minutes earlier each night and got to work 30 minutes sooner? You'd probably feel better, work better, and increase your income.

Hollywood is usually not a good place to look for examples. But some Hollywood executives who started out in the mailroom and ended up in the boardroom are good examples in terms of their dedication at the office.

Many of them started out by being the first one in the door and the last one out. More important than how many hours you work is how many important results you are creating for your organization. Be sure to spend 80% of your time on the 20% of your job that contributes most to the bottom line and well-being of your company.

As an experiment for a month, what would happen if you were the first one in (or arrived a half hour earlier than normal)? Try it for four weeks and see what happens. Your boss might have a heart attack...or your boss might give you a raise.

29 Is it a good idea to change jobs?

The first thing to change is your attitude about your current job. How can you bring more excellence and enthusiasm to it?

There is nothing wrong with changing jobs for the right reasons. Here are a few of them.

Change jobs when…

- *You are currently being asked to do something illegal or immoral.*

- *You cannot provide for yourself or your family in your current position.*

- *You have a clear opportunity to make more income and make a bigger difference for God's kingdom with a different job.*

- *God is calling you to a whole new line of work, e.g., owning your own business, working in a full-time ministry position, etc.*

Pray and ask God for direction. Ask Him to specifically confirm the best direction to you by opening doors or by closing doors. Did you know that God is more ready to guide us than we realize? God says that he will guide us and instruct us in the way that we are to go; that He will guide us by His eye. (Psalm 32: 8, 9) Do you remember when you were young how your parents guided you by "the look"? No words needed. We knew their directives, exactly. We also knew their look of pleasure and affirmation upon us. Oh, how God desires to guide His children.

30   How can I give myself a promotion?

Ready for a handy acrostic or acronym? Here's one that will help you get a promotion and/or increase in pay. It's the word **GROW**.

Give your company your very best. Ask your supervisor(s) for brutally honest feedback about the results you have been creating for the company.

Response-ability: Accept full responsibility for your actions. And if you are a team leader, be willing to take the responsibility for your team's results, too—even if a problem occurred that's not your fault. Also, learn to be responsive. If your organization is going through a crisis or a unique opportunity, respond (and help) accordingly.

Offer to expand what you do for the company in exchange for an increase in pay and/or a portion of the new revenue you create. What small business owner wouldn't welcome an employee saying, "If I can bring additional business to the firm, can I have a percentage of it?"

Welcome feedback. Invite input from your bosses and co-workers. Try to separate who you are as a person (remember that you are made in God's image and fully accepted in Christ) from what you do in the world of bottom-line results. Listen and look for ways that you can improve your contribution to the company.

If you are willing to **GROW** personally along these lines, your income will grow, too. It's a sure thing. You can't increase your value—for long—without increasing your income. It's one of God's laws. Keep sowing and you will reap.

Keep sowing and you will reap.

31 Can I save money by working from home?

Possibly! But watch out; you can also drive your family crazy. Here are a few pros and cons about working from home.

PROS

- *The commute is nice!*

- *You can work in your pajamas (though that is not recommended).*

- *You can write off many of your expenses on your taxes.*

- *You may have more time for work and family.*

CONS

- *You run the (very likely) risk of being constantly distracted by kids, the mail, noise, visitors, etc.*

- *You will have a harder time attracting professional employees, and you may limit your growth potential.*

- *The impression you give your customers may be: "amateur." And that's not good at all. When you have a separate place of business, your attitude and credibility in the work arena will likely be strengthened.*

32 Should I do good work for a mean boss?

Yes indeed. Here's why: Your real boss is not mean. He is perfect in every way.

You really work for God. So act like it. God didn't put you into your work environment by mistake. So do your best to make the best of it.

Here's one tip for making your boss nicer: Do good work for him or her!

And don't try to *talk* your boss into seeing your faith. Show it. As Jesus said, "Let your good deeds shine out for all to see, so that everyone will praise your Heavenly Father." (Matthew 5:16)

33 Should I keep working at a job where I don't get along too well with the people I work with?

Leo Tolstoy wrote: "Everyone thinks of changing the world, but no one thinks of changing himself."

Have you noticed that you can't change other people? It's a hard lesson, but the sooner we learn it, the better off we are. It's also nearly impossible to change yourself, but with God's help you can.

So how does this relate to your job? Simple. When you make changes in your attitude about the job, about your coworkers, and about your own work, you will notice that things will change. They have to. It's a scientific law that for every action (your improved attitude) there is a reaction (from your associates, customers, etc.).

Maybe you can tap into a little competitive spirit here. That's right. But do it God's way. Are your coworkers driving you nuts? Try:

- *Outserving them*

- *Outworking them*

- *Outcaring for them*

You will possibly win them over and you will certainly impress your supervisors. Here's the crucial thing: You cannot expect anything from them (but more whining). And remember, you might work with them, but you don't work for them – you work for God.

34 How can I get paid more for what I do?

By raising your fees or prices.

Obviously, that's easier to do if you own your own business. But you can have this mentality even as an employee. Here are the two things you need to do:

- *Do more than what you are paid for. Don't expect people to pay you more for doing or delivering less. This is where some people make a mistake. Give a greater value or service than you do now.*

- *Communicate to your customers or boss; educate them about the great service you are rendering for them. They may not be aware of how much you are helping them, saving them, or contributing to their well-being. So tell them.*

SAVINGS

*"I have enough money to last me the rest of my life—
unless I buy something."*

—JACKIE MASON

35   What's the best way to save money?

The best way to save money is to start today. There is no one special way. Being a good manager of God's money is important. Like a good farmer, you want to see a healthy harvest.

Hiding money in your pillowcase or under your bed is one form of saving. And it beats blowing your money on lottery tickets. But there are better ways to get a return on what God has entrusted to you.

A good, basic savings account at your bank that yields a small percentage of annual return is a decent way to start. Other ways that yield a higher return are:

- *Mutual funds*
- *Stocks and bonds*
- *Treasury bills*
- *Real estate investments*
- *And the list goes on*

Note: Life insurance, though highly recommended as a way to protect your family, is not a good investment or savings tool. A couple of decades ago, A.L. Williams turned the insurance world upside down with a great slogan: "Buy term (life insurance) and invest the difference." The point here was, and I think still is, that you should avoid whole life insurance. Buy term life insurance. Take the difference in cost and save or invest it.

More important than where you put your savings is how you save. Save regularly, and save systematically (the same time, the same way every month). Be sure to save.

36 How much should I save?

More than you do now. You should save a minimum of 10% of your income. That's a minimum. How can you do that? Here is the secret:

Make more and spend less.

Finding that 10% for your savings may not be as hard to do as you might imagine. For example, if you can make just 5% more each year (through raises, bonuses, side jobs, consulting, etc.) and spend just 5% less (eating out less often, cutting out soft drinks, buyig less merchandise, etc.) you will have that 10% and you'll hardly even feel it.

In terms of an emergency savings account, ideally you want to have one year's worth of income in savings. This should be in a liquid (meaning you-can-access-the-cash) savings account. Of course, most people don't have that much saved. Work toward having a minimum of three months' salary saved.

This will give you the freedom to look for another job if you need to. Or if, and this happens, you get laid off, you won't panic. Don't live check to check. That's not being wise with your income. Even the small creatures we share this earth with store up food for the winter season. So set aside at least three months' worth of money in your emergency savings account.

37 Should I still save money while I am in debt?

That is a great question. In a real sense, when you pay down your debt, you are saving money. You are saving money on high interest rates, late fees, and more.

There is another excellent book called *You'll Never Have Financial Freedom By Paying Off Your Debt* by Curt Whipple (you can order it at Amazon.com). Whipple's main idea is that you have to do both. If you only focus on paying down your debt, it's like you are eliminating a negative without building a positive (net worth).

What I recommend to my clients and friends is the 5 & 5 plan. Take that 10% you are saving and split it into two parts. Use half of it for debt reduction and the other half for savings.

For my really motivated clients, I recommend the 10 & 10 plan. This one will have you financially independent in a very short period of time. How do you do it? You guessed it: Save/invest 10% of your income. Reduce your debt with 10% of your income.

Wow! This means that you are living on just 70% of your income. Why's that? Because, remember, you put God (and giving to His work) number one. This means you set aside 10% or more right off the top for Him. I have seen God bless this plan time and again for those who trust Him.

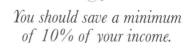

You should save a minimum of 10% of your income.

38 How much should I have saved before I get married?

More than you think!

In Biblical times, men took a year off work to tend to (and adjust to) their new brides. Guess what that means? They had at least a year's worth of savings to live on.

Another tip: Your wedding is an important day. But don't spend so much on that one day that you put yourself (or your parents) behind for years. It's just not worth it. Make it a wonderful celebration, not a status event.

Also remember that, as a couple, you may be in a better place financially than you were as singles. You can share living expenses, meals, travel costs, and more.

So if you have found the right person, and they are ready to share your life in God, don't let the lack of money hold you back.

WARNING! If the person you are dating is a shopoholic, a gambling addict, or has never held down a job, you need to save something else: Save yourself from disaster. Don't make the mistake so many people make. Don't you dare think that you will change your spouse when you are married. If anything, whatever habits that person has now, marriage will multiply them. You become more of what you already are when you marry. For example, if giving to God's work is important to you, make sure your future mate shares that value. And make sure they don't just agree with a nod. Are they currently tithing to God?

39 What is the power of "compound" interest?

In a nutshell, compound interest is the nearly miraculous fact that your money can earn interest on the interest it's earning. This is when your money works for you.

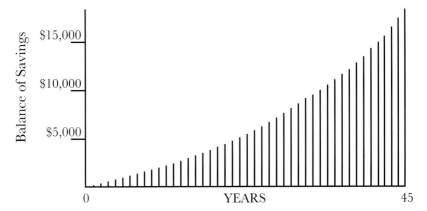

Compound Interest
$100 invested annually for 45 years at 5 % interest = $17,667

40 How can I benefit from compounding interest?

By starting immediately. There are a few keys to enjoying the fruit of compound interest:

- *The sooner you get started saving, the more amazing the results. See the above chart. Use an example like this to show your kids how exciting saving money is.*

- *The higher the interest rate the better. Note: Generally, the higher the rate of return, the higher the risk. So measure your goals in that area.*

- *The more you can deposit, the more you will see in terms of returns.*

- *Don't touch those deposits! Taking money out of savings (before it's time) is like taking a half-baked brownie out of the oven. Don't do it. You'll kill the compound-interest effect.*

So invest in savings as much as you can and as often as you can. You will be blown away at how compound interest will make more money from your money. This is one of the ways the rich get richer.

TAXES

"Ever notice that when you put the word 'The' and 'IRS' together, it spells 'THEIRS'?"

—JACKIE MASON

41 How can I save money on my taxes?

It's not as hard as you think. Here are some **ABC**s:

Accounting: Keep track of every dollar you spend and every dollar you make.

Be sure you stay current with the IRS. Pay your taxes on time. You don't want to get behind and have to deal with late payments, fees, or the dreaded liens on your property, bank levies, or wage garnishments.

Count every deduction you possibly can. It's wrong not to pay taxes (it is both unbiblical and illegal), but it is also poor stewardship not to look for every deduction you are entitled to take.

42 Where can I find the best tax breaks?

Let me count the ways…

- *Health-care benefits. You shouldn't pay this tax when your employer pays the premiums for your health insurance and health care.*

- *Contributions to retirement accounts.*

- *Lower rates on dividends and long-term capital gains.*

- *The mortgage-interest deduction.*

- *State and local income taxes and personal property taxes.*

- *Charitable contributions.*

- *Children under age 17. The child tax credit puts $1,000 per child in your pocket.*

- *The earned income credit. You may qualify for the earned income tax credit, which is targeted at low-income taxpayers.*

- *Life insurance or annuity contracts. There is no current tax on the inside investment income.*

If you are self-employed or own your own business, you are likely in a position to qualify for many other tax breaks. As always, discuss this with your tax professional.

43 Do I need a CPA?

I highly recommend that you get one. Of course, I am biased. I am a CPA. (Go to the back of this book to find out how to contact my office and for additional resources.)

A CPA is a Certified Public Accountant. This means that they are qualified to advise you in terms of your money, tax codes, and proper reporting procedures. There is a wonderful saying: "Success leaves clues."

Most financially successful people have a CPA on their team.

Chances are very good that your CPA will pay for himself or herself several times over in terms of helping you save money on your taxes, handling your tax planning, and by advising you on "money matters."

Read those last two words above one more time: Money matters. That's why it's important to have a professional CPA helping you make every dollar count.

44 What's the best way to file my taxes?

On time!

Other than that, there are many ways to file your tax returns. You can do it via the mail, and now even with the convenience of email.

Again, the important thing is that you file on time and file properly. If you do not have a CPA, you should at the very least file your taxes with a certified tax preparer.

You've heard the saying, "It takes money to make money," right? Well this is also true with your taxes. You might say, "It takes money to save money." So I want to recommend that you hire a successful tax preparer. It will cost you more than doing it yourself or at a small-based firm, but you will see the difference in the savings you get in terms of your higher deductions and lower tax liabilities.

45 Should I incorporate or become self-employed?

If you work full-time as an employee for a company, the answer is usually "No." However, if you work freelance, have a DBA ("doing business as") license, do consulting work, or anything else where you set your own hours and fees, then the answer is "Yes."

There are advantages to being self-employed. This is also called a "sole proprietorship." This means that you are the boss, the owner of the business. The main advantage is that you will have a tremendous opportunity for tax deductions, also happily referred to as write-offs. You might be surprised how many of your expenses are tax deductible when you are self-employed.

There is also an upside to incorporating your business. One of the main advantages is that you will have a legal "shield" that can protect your personal finances from lawsuits. The law treats a corporation as an entity of its own, almost like a person. You have several choices if you incorporate. You can become:

- *An LLC – this is a Limited Liability Company.*

- *An "S" Corp – this is often appropriate for a midsized company with an owner(s) highly active in the business.*

- *A "C" Corp – this offers the most protection and is generally for the larger companies, or a company intending to become much larger.*

Be sure to speak with a professional about your situation and what is best for you. A business or tax attorney can advise you and can also help you file appropriately.

46 How can I get out of the trouble I am in with the IRS?

One thing to stop doing immediately: *Stop ignoring the IRS.* If you have a problem, trust me (I am an IRS Problem Solver), it will not go away by itself.

Some things to start doing: Hire an expert to help you. Go to **www.YourIRSProblemSolvers.com** for starters. Make a payment plan with the IRS and start making payments on time every time. Consider doing an "offer and compromise" with the IRS.

Don't be intimidated by the IRS. This is a branch of the government, but remember government is "for the people." If you cooperate with them, you will get better results than you will by avoiding, covering up, or running from your problems. Be ethically aggressive. For example, did you know that you can amend your tax returns for the previous three years?

It's quite likely that you may have overpaid or understated your deductions on previous tax returns. You can file amended returns for previous years. One of my clients recently did this and saved $15,000 on his IRS bill.

47 Will the IRS let me make payments to them?

Yes, in many cases they will. Late payments are better than no payments. And you can often set up a payment plan called an installment agreement if you have fallen behind on your state or federal tax returns. But please keep in mind:

- *You want to have an installment agreement from the*

IRS. This is your go ahead to make those payments. It's a contractual agreement you make with the IRS.

- *You will likely have to pay extra in penalties and interest. Usually these are fairly reasonable. But if you can pay in full, it's best to do so.*

- *If you default on your payment plan, you can be in worse shape than when you started. Keep on top of it, and stay in close communication with the IRS.*

 ## Is it wrong to cheat a little bit on my taxes?

Yes, it is.

You are frustrated with the government. I am, too. But this doesn't give us the right to do wrong.

How do we know that it is wrong to cheat on our taxes? Because God says, "You shall not steal." (Exodus 20:15) He did not qualify that with "except from organizations that frustrate you."

Be aggressive on your tax returns, but be honest. Take advantage of tax avoidance not tax evasion. Report your income. Make sure your tax deductions are legitimate. You may get audited at some point (keep your records for seven years).

As a matter of fact, you will get audited by a much higher authority than the IRS. God, Himself, will ask you to give an account of how you managed His money.

49 Should I barter my services?

First let me explain what that means. Bartering is when you exchange your products or services for someone else's. Usually there is no cash exchanged. It's about trading with others for things you want or need.

On the "for" side: You can often get services or items you want at a far lower actual cost by doing this. This is because you are exchanging something you make or provide, which costs you little (or nothing) for something that you normally have to pay top dollar to get. Also, there are bartering clubs and associations you can join. You can save a ton of money and obtain things you normally wouldn't be able to afford.

On the "against" side: Alan Weiss, the consultant to consultants, once said, "Bartering is for farmers." What I think he meant was that we no longer live in the kind of world where most people will benefit much from this type of exchanging. It can become a distraction from your core business. Plus, you may end up with things you wouldn't have normally wanted or needed in the first place, just because you thought you were getting "such a good deal."

There is no right or wrong on this one. Be aware though that in most cases, if you do decide to barter, you will still have tax consequences to deal with. But they may be far lower than if you were making cash sales or purchases.

GIVING

"Give More, Make More, Save More"
—PHIL LIBERATORE

50 | What should I do with the money I do have?

The natural thought process when considering money is: to make more, save more, give more. Based upon my understanding and experience of Scriptural principles, I believe that the first imperative is to give more. Yes, my suggestion is: Put giving first!

You can earn God's way—through serving others. You can save and invest the money God has generously given to you. And, perhaps most importantly, you can give to God's work, His people, and those in need.

Next, understand that just as "Your life is not your own," neither is your money. God has entrusted you with it. He wants to see if you will be faithful to Him with your finances. Remember the words of Jesus, "Whoever sows sparingly will also reap sparingly, and whoever sows generously will also reap generously. Each man should give what he has decided in his heart, not reluctantly or under compulsion, for God loves a cheerful giver. And God is able to make all grace abound to you, so that in all things at all times, having all that you need, you will abound in every good work." (2 Corinthians 9:6-9)

Be faithful with what you've got. Share it! Give it to God's work. You'll be blessed for it.

51 How much should I give to God?

The answer might surprise you. Do you think it's 10%? 20%? Not even close. Give God all of it! Does that mean you need to write a check to your church or charity for all of the money in your possession? Probably not. It means that God wants all of you, and that includes your money. Giving 10% of your income to God's work is a good start.

Here's a handy acronym to help you remember some of God's principles about giving. It's the word **CHEER** and it reminds us that God loves a cheerful giver:

> **<u>C</u>ontribute** to God's work.
> **<u>H</u>appily** give your tithes and offerings to God.
> **<u>E</u>quip** God's people through your giving.
> **<u>E</u>vangelize** with your giving to help fulfill the Great Commission.
> **<u>R</u>each** out to those in need. And don't forget to give thanks…with a grateful heart.

52 Who should get the money I give to God?

You should bless those who bless you. First stop: your local church. The New Testament is clear that those who spend their lives preaching the gospel should make their living from the gospel.

God is also crystal clear that we should look out for widows and orphans. Jesus' brother, James, even wrote, "This is true religion." (James 1:27)

Feeding the poor is not an option. We haven't been given the option of opting out of that. You can allocate some of your giving specifically to a ministry like The Salvation Army or World Vision. Or perhaps your church has specific ministries for these various areas of need.

God has not told us to "retreat." He wants to "advance" His Kingdom through the Good News of the Gospel of Jesus Christ. Support Mission organizations like Campus Crusade, Far East Broadcasting, The Billy Graham organization, World Vision, and others that God may put on your heart.

When you are in doubt, do these three things:

- *Pray and ask God for wisdom.*

- *Make sure you are involved in a Christ-honoring, Bible-believing church.*

- *Give to your local church. They pass the plate or offering basket each Sunday, right? Don't miss the opportunity to give!*

53　Should I pay a "tithe" or portion of my income to God?

Many Christians believe that the idea of "tithing," or giving 10% of your income to God, is an Old Testament idea. Here are a few thoughts about that:

First, nowhere in the New Testament does Jesus or any of the Apostles say to stop tithing.

Second, if you feel that this requirement has been set aside, you have to ask yourself the following question: Does God expect us to be more or less generous in the New Covenant than Old Testament saints were in the Old Covenant?

A good rule of thumb is to do both. Tithe to your local church, and give above and beyond that to Christ-centered ministries and those in need.

Tithing is a great, Biblical habit you can learn. Ask people who tithe consistently if God has blessed them and their finances. Guess what? You are going to get "Yes!" answers. God guarantees it in Malachi 3:10!

54 Is it OK to give to more than one ministry?

Certainly, it is! The more (you give) the merrier (you'll be).

In a certain sense, there is only one ministry: The ongoing work of sharing the Good News about Jesus Christ.

Of course, that "sharing" comes in many forms. If someone is hungry and their stomach is growling so loud they can't hear the words you are saying, should you start preaching to them? Of course not.

The church is central to God's plan for human beings. But remember that the church is more than just an organization. It is a living, breathing organism. You and I are God's church.

When you give to Biblical ministries this book describes, whether that is through one ministry or many, e.g., para-church organizations, you are giving to the Lord. But please do not neglect your local church. It takes money to keep those lights on so that His light can be proclaimed.

The more you give, the happier you'll be.

If you need additional ideas about what kinds of ministries need support, check out **www.ecfa.org**, a web site that introduces Christian givers to various ministries.

55 How can I know which ministries are legitimate?

Avoid any "ministry" that does not acknowledge Jesus as Lord. Don't give them a dime or a second look. Now does that mean you should never give to a non-Christian? Not at all. At that point, you are the minister. Just be careful about inadvertently helping cultists or others who are opposed to the Lord of Glory.

Here are three other helpful guidelines to consider before giving to a ministry:

- *Do they have a Biblical statement of faith?*

- *Are they accountable to a local church and/or a Christian body of directors?*

- *Can they show you exactly how the funds are to be used?*

God doesn't want us to judge or condemn others. But we must be "fruit inspectors." If a ministry is asking you for money, but they have no Biblical fruit to show for their efforts, go to another fruit stand.

Note: This doesn't always mean that the ministries you support have to have big numbers. It means that it is crucial

Avoid any "ministry" that does not acknowledge Jesus as Lord.

that you give to God-honoring work. Entrust your giving to people who trust in Christ and want to please Him.

56 There are so many worthy causes. Which ones should I support?

Here is an important principle: Don't just give where you feel the need; give where you believe God has called you to give.

Even Jesus did not heal everybody in Israel. He was called to minister to certain people and He faithfully did just that. You have been called, too. There are three keys to knowing how to choose:

- *Where has God placed you?*

- *What has God placed on your heart?*

- *Who has God put in your path?*

There are no accidents or coincidences with God. When you ask Him to direct your steps, He will lead you to the ministries and ministers He has called you to support.

Oh, and one more thing: He has also called you to be a minister right where you are. Maybe you are in a position where God, through His people, wants to support the work you are doing for His sake.

57 Should I support missionaries?

Yes! In fact, if God has called you to stay, he's called you to pay. What I mean is every Christian is commanded to support the Great Commission of spreading the Gospel of Jesus Christ around the world.

If you can't physically "go" into all the world, you can still help spread the Good News by supporting Christian missionaries. Here are a few guidelines:

- *Make sure the missionaries you support are spreading the real Gospel (I Corinthians 15:1-5).*

- *Make an effort to support the missionaries your local church is sponsoring. They are an extended part of your church family.*

- *Make a strong attempt to do some missions work yourself. Can't make it to Africa for ten years? How about going to Mexico for two weeks next summer? You don't speak Indonesian? OK. How about working with your inner-city mission in the town where you live?*

58 What does it mean to give with a cheerful heart?

It means that you give, without obligation or duty! The key is not your financial position. It's the position of your heart. "God loves a cheerful giver." (2 Corinthians 9:7) Here's a **GLAD** acronym that will help you give cheerfully.

Give thanks before you give anything else.

Laugh and enjoy giving to God, simply because you love Him.

Accept that every good thing comes from God above and rejoice in Him.

Don't hold back. Take a look at the word "stingy." It'll sting you. Give generously to God and others, even when you don't feel like it. Act as if you are cheerful, and soon you will be.

59 How can I receive God's blessings?

The first thing you must do is to understand that God blesses in many ways. He blesses us with hope in Him, with forgiveness, with life, with family and friends, and He blesses us financially.

So right off the bat, you should give thanks for the ways God has already blessed you.

If you believe you are stuck in a spiritual rut and are not experiencing God's blessing, it is possible that God is disciplining you as His son or daughter.

This doesn't always feel good. But it's good for you. God is pruning you. He is shaping your character. God cares more about your character than he does about your bank account.

Finally, God blesses us by our obedience to His commands and laws. God's love for you will never change. He loves you with an everlasting love. But, His ability to bless you comes by your obedience to His percepts.

60 How can I experience the law of sowing and reaping?

You are experiencing it every day!

That's like asking, "How can I experience the law of gravity?" You can't help but obey the law of gravity. Try walking up the side of a building sometime. Unless you are Spiderman, it won't work out too well for you.

So the question really becomes, how can you experience the blessings that come from proper sowing and reaping?

Here are **Three P's** to help you with this:

Plant the right kinds of seeds. You will get more of whatever you sow.

Put as many seeds into the soil as you can. If you want a big harvest, you need to not only plant the right kinds of seeds, but also plant lots of them.

Persist in planting, nurturing, and watering seeds. Imagine if a farmer planted one or two seeds of corn, didn't see any crop, and just gave up. No. Keep planting. As the Bible says, "In due time we will reap if we do not grow weary." (Galatians 6:9)

61 How can I develop good money habits?

It starts by defining specifically what good money habits are. Some of the best ones we have outlined in this book include:

- *The habit of giving from the heart.*

- *The habit of saving systematically.*

- *The habit of sowing and reaping on purpose.*

There is only one way to create strong habits in any area of your life, including managing your money. Here it is: REPETITION.

Give each week. Save each week. Sow seeds in good soil each week. Experts in human behavior have pointed out that it usually takes 21 days to incorporate a new habit into your life. So avoid the trap of trying to learn too many new habits all at once.

As you go through this book, highlight some of the principles and suggestions that seem especially relevant to your life. Then pick the top three. Next, narrow it down to the one thing you think you should start with first.

Make that one thing a habit for a month, and then move down the list to number two, and then number three. Make your habits carefully because they will end up making (or breaking) you.

62 Should I still give, even when I hardly have enough for myself?

Yes. One of the reasons you hardly have enough may very well be because you aren't giving to God and others. And please note that you can give in many ways. Give of your time. Give of your expertise. Give your possessions. Give someone a listening ear.

There was a time in my life when I was unemployed. My wife and I agreed to continue giving to our church. The Lord blessed us. Within seven months, God enabled me to start my own tax accounting practice. Today, we have more than 3,500 clients.

Too many people wait till they "have enough" before they want to start giving. The problem is, when is enough ever really enough? When Rockefeller was the richest man in the world, somebody once asked him, "How much money do you need, Mr. Rockefeller?" He answered, "A little more."

> *There are many ways of giving—giving money is but one of the different ways.*

So hand it over. Not just your money. Hand over your heart, mind, soul, and strength to God. Watch and see. God will bless you. He will give you the ability to have and give even more.

63 How do you store up treasures in heaven?

By investing in God's work here on earth.

All of life is spiritual because we are made in God's image and we live in His creation. What Jesus said about storing up treasure in Heaven is another take on the principle of sowing and reaping. When you:

- *Seek first God's kingdom (Matthew 6:33)*

- *Give to God's work and His people*

- *Spread the Good news of the Gospel*

you may not always see an earthly return on that investment, but you will see a return. The Bible says that God is not mocked, and "whatever a man sows, that also will he reap." So if you sow these good things on Earth, you will reap rewards in Heaven.

I'll see you there. It's going to be great! Keep an eternal perspective!

64 People owe me money and don't pay me back. What should I do?

Why am I putting this question about loaning money in the giving section of he book?

Never loan money you can't afford to lose. Here's why: Many times you will lose it. A loan is not a boomerang; it may not come back to you.

This is one of the reasons why credit card companies charge such exorbitant interest rates. You are paying for all of the other guys who neglect to pay.

My advice is to make these loans out of your giving budget. Don't think of a loan as a financial investment. Think of it as a personal investment in someone's life.

If you must make a loan and need to get repaid, I recommend two things:

- *Put your loan in writing. Be very clear about the specifics. How much money was loaned? When is it due? Whom is it payable to? What happens if the money is paid back late? Is there interest on the loan?*

- *Have your loan paper signed by both parties as an agreement and have it notarized. Make sure you keep a copy in case you end up in small claims court (not good) or mediation (better).*

INSURANCE AND ESTATE PLANNING

"There once was a very cautious man, who never laughed or cried. He never cared; he never dared; he never dreamed or tried. And when one day he passed away, his insurance was denied. For since he never really lived, they claimed he never died."

—ANONYMOUS

65 Should I buy life insurance? What's the best kind?

I think so. I used to think that you didn't need it because you should "just trust God."

We need to trust God, but we also need to be trustworthy servants for God. Look out for your family. God has promised you eternal life, but He has not told you how many days of earthly life you have left.

I recommend that you have at least a $500,000 policy of life insurance with your spouse as the main beneficiary (and director of your estate).

As was mentioned previously, I recommend term life insurance over whole life.

66 What other kinds of insurance should I get?

It depends on one key; where are you vulnerable?

- *You may be required to have car insurance in your state or province. Whether you have to or not, get some. And have enough to cover the possibility that the guy who hits you may not have any insurance.*

- *If you can afford it, purchase health insurance with a high deductible. In the U.S., I prefer PPO to HMO, because I want the freedom to choose the doctor or specialist who is right for me. Go to the doctor for regular check-ups, but avoid running up your medical bills just to meet your deductible. Remember, doctors are in business to make money. (The good ones also care about your health.)*

- *If you have a business, be sure to look into liability insurance. You can't afford to have one of your employees or vendors put you under because of negligence. I recommend at least a $1,000,000 liability policy to cover you and your business, even at the start-up level.*

67 How do I create a Will or Living Trust?

If you want to do it yourself, there are forms available right in your local public library. You can also go to dozens of websites for help.

For example, check out: **www.doyourownwill.com**. This is a resource you can access to get started online right away.

If you don't have a will, you really should get one. Even if you don't have much in the way of assets (yet), it is important that you leave clear-cut directions for your loved ones to follow.

You can even handwrite a basic "Last Will and Testament" sheet. Sign it. Have a notary sign it.

But in today's world, you really should have more than that. Go over this important concern with your attorney.

God has given you life. Be sure that you glorify Him when it's time to meet Him. For example, did you know that you can leave some of your estate to your church or other ministry you want to support? Do it.

68 Can I count on getting Social Security?

Not really. You can count on death and taxes. And you can count on going to Heaven if you have a personal relationship with God through Jesus Christ.

We don't really know about the future of Social Security.

> *The problem is that we are now at the point where money is flowing out of Social Security.*

It's probably best to think about it as dessert and not as your main course. If it comes, that's nice, but if it doesn't, you won't go hungry.

Again, there's nothing wrong with getting Social Security. You paid into it and you should be paid out from it. The problem, as I'm sure you know, is that we are now at the point where more money is flowing out of Social Security than will be coming in.

Depend on God, and invest and save wisely for your future. It's more likely that the government will take away than give in the future.

69 How can I leave income for my children after I die?

Glad you asked. Giving your children an inheritance is a Biblical idea and you should plan ahead for it.

If they are not adults yet, you should plan in your will or Living Trust to leave it with a designated Beneficiary. This role should be given to someone you trust to look out for your kids.

Also, be careful about leaving too much money in the hands of your kids if they are young or still immature. You won't be doing them any favors if you give them more than they can handle or give it at the wrong time in their lives.

Think and plan these things through with your attorney. And remember that you should also plan ahead to support your church and other charities in your inheritance. Plan on using term life insurance as the primary vehicle for leaving your kids with ongoing support.

And remember the old Christian Latin expression: "Memento Mori." This means remember that you are mortal. Make your life on earth count, and think and pray ahead about what's best for your kids.

70 How soon can I retire?

Not as soon as you think—unless you plan for it! Here's an acronym to help you plan ahead. You guessed it, the word is **RETIRE**:

Relax now. Don't wait until you're retired to rejuvenate your life. You can retire from stress by "casting all of your cares upon Him." While you are in this state of meditation and relaxation, go ahead and…

Estimate your ideal retirement age. No one can do this for you. For some people this is 55, for others it is 85. But the goal is to set the date you want instead of being forced to work to manage your debt load or pay for your standard of living.

Take stock of how much income you'll need at that age. This is a best guesstimate. But you need to have an amount in mind so that you can…

Invest in a plan that will automatically pay you that monthly amount of income when you reach your ideal retirement age.

Regularly contribute to your savings and investment portfolio. Do this habitually and you will ensure a secure retirement.

Enjoy your retirement, but don't check out of living. Use this opportunity to volunteer, spend time with your grandkids, or turn your hobby into a business. Have fun and be faithful.

71 How much life insurance do I really need?

Here's a rule of thumb I like to use:

Take your annual income and multiply it by ten. If you currently make $50,000 per year, you need a $500,000 life insurance policy. If you are making $100,000 per year, take out a $1,000,000 life insurance policy.

Calculate how much life insurance you need by multiplying your annual income by ten.

This is especially true if you are the sole or primary money-earner for your family. Remember that if you were to pass away unexpectedly, your family would have major costs, adjustments, taxes, and expenses to deal with.

Make sure that you replace your income for more than just the first two or three years you will be gone. Again, I think term insurance is the best approach for this. You can shop for great term quotes online now.

72 What is the first step toward financial independence?

The first step of any journey begins with two questions:

- *Where am I going?*

- *What's the best way to get there?*

So start by defining "financial independence." Does this mean you never have to work a regular job again? Is it having one million dollars in the bank? Is it eliminating all of your debt?

Here's something you should know. By the standard of human history, you already are rich. Did you know that? You will live longer, enjoy more material things, see more of the world, and enjoy better health than the richest of the rich who lived just a hundred years ago.

So that's another thing to be grateful for. Plus, you will enter Heaven with all of your debts paid for in full by Jesus Christ. (Isaiah 53:4-6)

FAMILY BUDGET

"Knowing is not enough; we must apply.
Willing is not enough; we must do."
—JOHANN VON GOETHE

73 What is a good way I can lower my monthly expenses?

The first thing is to be honest, brutally honest with yourself, and your spouse. Are you confusing things you want with things you truly need? Here's an exercise that can help you lower your expenses:

First, make a careful list of all of your monthly expenses. Then total them up.

Next, eliminate 20% of the money total. So if your monthly expenses are $10,000, take $2,000 off. Now go back and refigure your true, hard expenses and budget in such a way that you pay for those products and services for $8,000 per month instead of $10,000. If you can't get those items for less, begin cutting out or down the things that are not necessities (clothes, bowling, movies, etc.).

Finally, go back (if you really need to) and put back 10%

———— ❧ ————

The best way to lower month-
ly expenses is to be brutally
honest with yourself.

———— ❧ ————

of the money; in this case, $1,000. You may find that you can get by without putting it back. Most people can get by on 80% of their income. But you can take the 10% and re-insert it—if you feel you must. This way, you still have cut your monthly expenses/budget down by 10%.

74

How much money should I give my kids?

When it comes to money and teaching your kids how to be wise with it, the sooner they earn it, the better they learn it.

My wife and I have two wonderful daughters. Our perspective is that their allowance is theirs, just because we love them. It is a reasonable, modest amount. Extra money can be earned by doing odd jobs like baby-sitting or extra chores around the house.

There is no set amount that you should give or not give your kids. The key is to remember that, just like your money, your kids don't really belong to you—they belong to God. Your job is to help them become dependent on God and not on you. And you will do this primarily by your example. They won't always listen to what you say, but they will watch what you do. So make sure that you are plugged into a local church and supporting the ministry with your time, talents, and giving.

Most importantly, teach your children to tithe. When our daughters started getting an allowance, we ordered personal tithe envelopes from our church with their own tithe number. Weekly, we taught them to set aside 10% of their allowance for tithe, 5% for church offering, 10% for giving gifts to family and friends, and 10% to a savings account. We encouraged them to use the other 65% to save up for something they really wanted to purchase or to use it as they chose. In this way, they were able to have the joy of placing their tithe and offering into the offering plate and experience worship in giving. They were also able to experience the gratification of opening up a savings account and making deposits, periodically. They also knew that when they gave gifts to others, it was truly coming from their heart, because it came from their own pocket book. We feel that this was great preparation for developing godly stewardship of money in their lives.

75 Should I send my kids to private Christian schools?

I do. But you need to think and pray this through with your spouse. Here's what is most important:

God has given you as the parent the responsibility of raising and training (that includes educating) your children. Nowhere in the Bible is the state or the church given this commandment.

There are godly people with kids who are home schooled, going to private Christian schools, and going to public schools. The key is for you to understand that whoever you have educating your kids is your responsibility, and if you can't do the home-school route, you are delegating this responsibility to others. That's OK. Delegating is a good thing. Just be wise about it.

And remember, you cannot educate kids in a moral vacuum. It's impossible. And there really is no neutrality when it comes to values. Personally, my kids have blossomed within the setting of Christian education. If I had to choose between a smaller house and having my kids go to a Christ-honoring school, guess what? We're moving to a smaller house.

But you need to make this decision prayerfully. Your kids are worth it!

76 What are the categories that make up a budget?

Here's a basic sample budget for personal finances:

- ❏ Housing
- ❏ Utilities
- ❏ Home and cell phones
- ❏ TV/Cable
- ❏ Transportation
- ❏ Food
- ❏ Personal insurance and pensions
- ❏ Personal taxes
- ❏ Computer & Internet
- ❏ Entertainment
- ❏ Apparel products and services
- ❏ Health care
- ❏ Miscellaneous expenses
- ❏ Education
- ❏ Personal care products and services
- ❏ Cash Contributions
- ❏ Church Giving
- ❏ Books
- ❏ Savings
- ❏ Giving Fund
- ❏ Total

The most important thing is not which type of budget you use, the key is that you use one. Find one that works and start working it. You'll be so glad you did.

How can I work with my spouse to solve my financial problems?

Very carefully and very lovingly.

More than likely, one spouse will take the lead on handling the finances, paying the bills, monitoring bank accounts, etc. The key to working together is to always be in communication on financial decisions. You've heard it said never use words like "never" and "always" in communication? Perhaps this is where the exception lies. Develop a shared vision and always be in agreement; never make financial decisions without communicating with your spouse.

Remember that God has put your partner into your life to teach you to be holy. Holiness is more important to God than happiness (happiness follows holiness). Here are seven things to agree upon together:

- *Financial goals*
- *A budget*
- *Giving goals*
- *A savings and investment plan*
- *Education for your children*
- *Home ownership*
- *Life insurance and a will*

These are the most important areas to discuss. But the most vital word is that word "together." Staying together and working together is more important than having your way about the budget, for example. Serve one another and do all that you can to communicate (even if you need a counselor or pastor to help). Develop a shared vision.

78 Is it better to buy a new car or a used one?

It's almost always better to buy a used one for the following reasons:

- *As soon as you drive off a new car lot, your car goes down in value thousands of dollars. That's an expensive first drive.*

- *Cars, in most cases, unlike homes do not appreciate in value. They depreciate. So think of your car as an expense, not an investment.*

- *With a good warranty and service plan, a two-year-old car will look, drive, and operate like new.*

And please remember, just like with buying a house, when you buy a car, you are also purchasing the loan you get. Make sure it's one you can live with. Better yet, pay cash for your car. This will also help you negotiate a lower price.

And when it comes to buying a car, keep in mind that your best negotiating advantage is your willingness to walk right off the dealership lot. Don't ever get pressured into buying a vehicle you don't need or can't afford.

79 Are college loans a good idea?

A better question might be, "Is college a good thing?" And which colleges are the best?

Much of this depends on your college student. (Or if you are a college student reading this book—and I commend you—it depends on your unique situation).

If you decide to pay your son or daughter's way, I highly recommend that you hold them accountable for a solid grade-point average. But back to the question of loans...

The rates on student loans are very competitive. If you look at college as a necessary or strategic investment, you could justify taking out a college loan. For example, going to a law school and paying for it with student loans might be justifiable if you are confident that you can get a good return on that investment when you pass the bar and begin billing clients as an attorney.

Make sure that your college student pays their own way as much as possible. This will give your student critical life experience and will help him or her value their education. This payment might come through scholarships, paid internships, part-time work, or full-time work in the summer.

INVESTMENTS

"Behind me is infinite power. Before me is infinite possibility. Around me is endless opportunity. Why should I fear?"

—ANONYMOUS

80 What does the saying "Let money work for you" mean?

Most people work for money (meaning to get it, and they don't). Financially successful people let money work for them (meaning that they allow money to grow, and it does).

If you are spending your money on things that don't last, e.g., entertainment, clothes, and expensive dinners, you are not putting your money to work.

You'll begin to see money working for you, even while you sleep, when you have invested your money into giving, savings, and investments. And this is exactly what God wants you to do with the money He puts in your care.

God wants you to give, save, and invest.

81 Should I invest in real estate?

Probably. It's a real good way to go. In fact, real estate has helped more people become well-to-do than any other single form of investment.

Some of Robert Kiyosaki's books are helpful here. Kiyosaki is the author of *Rich Dad, Poor Dad* and several other excellent books. You can, of course, also buy the "no money down" types of courses, but be aware: Many of those are get-rich-quick schemes. And the only people who get rich quick from them are the infomercial creators.

You can invest in real estate funds, you can buy rental property, and you can invest in land. You can start by buying your own home. And remember the three time-tested rules about real estate. Are you ready for them? Here they are:

Location!

Location!

Location!

82 Should I invest in the stock market?

There is no right or wrong answer to this question. Historically, the stock market has been a good investment. But here are some tips for you if you decide to get into the market:

- *Get in and stay in. Don't expect an immediate return.*

- *Diversify, Diversify, and Diversify.*

- *Look for long-term trends and invest in funds or companies that have positioned themselves accordingly.*

For example, at the time of this writing, investing in oil is a good move. Supplies go down and prices go up. It looks like it will be that way for the foreseeable future.

However, you also want to think long term about things like alternative energy, the aging baby-boomer population, etc. Make sure you work with a professional broker. You can learn a lot and then venture out on your own. But make sure you have a good coach (financial advisor) before you step out on this court.

83 Should I buy government bonds?

Let's face facts here. We don't know the future. But as believers in Christ, we know the One who holds the future.

Government bonds are as good as the government that prints them. Here in the U.S.A., this has been a good investment. Again, it's a long-term investment. You will get a better return than you would in a traditional bank account.

There are more aggressive ways to invest your money. But this may be a good place to start getting a higher yield on your savings. Note: Municipal bonds are tax free.

84 Should I buy a house or rent?

Probably buy. But...

You should also ask this question: Which is wiser for you at this time? Long term, owning a home is the wise thing because home values generally appreciate faster than the interest rate you are paying.

However, maybe God is calling you to the mission field. Maybe it would be smarter for you to use your "seed money" to start the business God has equipped you to build.

So it might be better to rent for now and buy later. Most people don't own their homes anyway. The bank does. So the secret is to seek God's will, follow His principles for giving and saving, and then decide accordingly.

Owning a home may be the American Dream but it may not be your dream and it may not be God's plan for your or His timing. We have owned two homes in the twenty-six year span of our marriage. In each purchase we waited on the Lord's timing. We prayed and fasted and asked God to confirm the purchases to us in very specific ways. There were several homes that we pursued, but the Lord was faithful to answer our prayers and close those opportunities and open the purchases that He guided us to make. Ask Him! He will definitely show you!

85 What interest rate should I pay on my house?

The simple answer is: The lowest rate possible. But the answer is not always that simple. Look carefully at various home loan options. Read the fine print. If you don't understand it, find a professional who does and have them explain it to you.

It's important to know that you are not just buying a house, you are buying a home loan. Be aware of:

- *Whether your rate is adjustable.*

- *Do you have a prepayment penalty? (This can affect your ability to refinance the loan later.)*

- *Is your rate for 10, 20, 30, or 40 years?*

Look at the interest rate, but also look at the big picture. What are you really buying into with this loan? Does it help your family accomplish your goals? Will it help you solve your financial problems, or will it create bigger ones?

86 Should I pay off my home mortgage early?

It's amazing how quickly you can actually do it. There are some real advantages here:

- *The interest on your house payments is tax deductible.*

- *You can cut the length of your mortgage down, way down.*

- *You can have, and have access to, the full equity in your home.*

If you can do this, go for it. There are many new home loans, at favorable rates, that can help you speed up this process. But you can also do this with your current loan.

For example, if you have a 30-year mortgage of $350,000 and your monthly payment is $2,200, here's how it might look for you. If you pay an extra $500 per month toward the principal, you will pay off your loan almost 11 years early! And you will save more than $191,000 in interest.

87 Do I need an IRA?

You don't necessarily need one, but it might be a good idea to set one up, especially if it's done through your employer. There are some real pluses to an IRA:

- *The "miracle" of compound interest will multiply your savings.*

- *You get a significant write-off on your taxes.*

- *You can defer tax payments until you reach the maturation point.*

- *You can set up your fund so that deposits are made automatically.*

- *There are more aggressive ways to invest your money, but there are few ways that are more sure-fire or advantageous to beginning investors than an IRA savings plan.*

———— ❧ ————

Set up an IRA, especially if it's done through your employer.

———— ❧ ————

88 Do I need a financial planner?

Yes.

But just as important as having an individual planner is having a PLAN. You plan where you're going to have lunch, where you will get your haircut, even where you will be buried, so why not plan for how you will reach your financial goals.

That reminds me: The most important starting point is having a financial goal. In fact, having many of them. What is your giving goal? Your earning goal? Your savings goal? Your retirement goal? Your vacation goal? Here are some more tips about financial planning:

- *Make sure your plan is in WRITING.*

- *Make sure you UNDERSTAND your plan and how to implement it.*

- *Make sure that you REVIEW and REVISE your plan frequently. I'd say at least two times a year.*

I do indeed recommend that you work with a professional financial planner. Ask them for at least three references. If they can't give you the names of several people they have helped make more, save more, and give away more, don't hire them.

GETTING AHEAD IN BUSINESS

"The only thing that stands between a man and what he wants in life is often merely the will to try it and the faith to believe that it is possible."

—DAVID VISCOTT

89 How can I earn more money?

Here's a modern business term for a Biblical idea: create value. This means that you will be paid in direct proportion to the specific contribution you make to your company or your customers.

Are you serious about making more? Do more. Serve more. Work smarter. Grow your company's reputation and profits.

Another thing to do is to start your own full- or part-time business. There is nothing sinful or shady about becoming a business or salesperson. In fact, in North America, nothing happens in the economy until somebody sells something to somebody else. What can you sell that is of service to others? Your expertise? Your labor? Your technology? Your new way of doing something that saves time and money?

There's a famous motivational book called *Think and Grow Rich*. Some people want the rich part without having to do the thinking part. Think about how you can contribute to others. And don't be afraid to charge them a fair price for it. There's nothing wrong with that.

Also, keep your overhead low. Do you need three TV sets? Can you get by driving that old car one more year? How about a vacation to a destination where you can also get involved in a missionary endeavor?

90 How can I make more income without sacrificing quality time with my family?

It's not as hard as it might sound. I have worked 20 years of extended hours from January to April 15th, which we affectionately call "tax season." This is a very demanding time, yet my family tells me that they didn't feel that they were disregarded or neglected, because I purposed that they were a priority and scheduled quality time with them. Establish regular times with your spouse or children. Make sure that God and your family are priorities in your life.

Next, cut out several time wasters. Let's be honest here. You, like most North Americans, probably watch the TV for a minimum of ten hours a week. Minimum. Am I right?

What if you used those ten-plus hours to make your hobby a part-time job, to write that book you've been meaning to write, to work at that restaurant a couple of nights a week, to address envelopes?

You have exactly all the time there is. The question is: How are you using it? Eliminate one or two unproductive things in your life, and find ways to increase your income.

Then find or create a job that helps other people and pays you, too.

91 How do I start my own business?

Start by doing something you have a passion for. This is crucial! How miserable it would be to get up every day and go perform a job in which you have no interest. I tell my employees, you've got to love what you are doing or start looking for something else. Work is such an adventure when you are passionate about what you are doing. Then utilize these ideas.

- *Have a vision and be able to cast it to others.*

- *Set your business up so that it's purpose-driven and provides service beyond your customer's expectation.*

- *Work on your business, not in it.*

- *Set your business up so that it's process-driven and not personality-driven. This is a key distinction.*

- *Create operating procedures for everything you do.*

But all of this presupposes one important thing. You must bring a valuable product or service to people. I happen to do tax and accounting because it is the best avenue for me to fulfill my passion, which is helping people.

And just as importantly, you must do a super job of marketing your business. Read as many marketing books as you can.

Finally, if you have the vision for a new biz, go for it. Write out exactly what it will take to not only conceive it, but also to manage and operate your business. Have a plan.

92 They say, "It takes money to make money." How can I find some start-up money?

The best way to find some start-up money is to save for it. This way you are not indebted to a rich uncle or the government.

Finding the money is not your biggest problem. There are hundreds of companies hoping you'll borrow their money. They will make back thousands and thousands more than they loan you.

Your real challenge is knowing how to best use that money. This is why a business plan is a great thing:

First, it will tell you whether you have a viable business.

Second, you can use it to attract a business partner or investors.

Third, it will give you a blueprint for operating your business.

One more thought. You may not need as much seed money as you think. If you use low cost/high response forms of advertising, i.e., word of mouth, referrals, and the Internet, you may be able to finance your way as you go.

One final note, the best avenue to having start-up money is to get started and make certain that you are providing the most excellent service possible. The greatest momentum that can be developed for the most growth is happy clients who feel cared for and valued. The greatest growth that I have experienced as a CPA has come through referrals.

93 What's the best type of business to get into?

The kind you love!

Maybe you heard about the book titled *Do What You Love and the Money Will Follow*. What a great line. And it's true. If you do what you love, you'll never "work" another day in your life.

One good indicator of the type of business, or the right role within a business for you, can come when you take the **DISC** personality test. It's fun and easy to take this test. You may be a:

Dominant Personality. This is not a bad thing. Each of these are God-given personality types. If you have this type of personality, you are a take-charge person. You might be a good entrepreneur, sales manager, or supervisor.

Influencer. You like to persuade people if you are in this category. Writing might be your thing, or public speaking. Sales may be another area where you shine.

Steady. If this describes you, you might be the go-to steady Eddy (or steady Betty) when it comes to work. You can be counted on. You are not known for creating drama. You get things done and you bring calm to the job.

Compliant. You like to make, keep, and enforce the rules. Accounting or bookkeeping might be your thing. You might be a good franchisee because you would be adept at following the franchise company's operating systems.

Find the type of work or business that connects to your God-given strengths. God has designed for you to prosper in the gifts and talents that he has given to you.

94 Is it a good idea to buy a franchise business?

Many times it is. Here's why:

With a franchise business, i.e., Subway, KFC, UPS store, all of the business "bugs" have already been worked out of the system. Your main concern becomes operating their proven, winning formula.

A few notes:

- *90% of new businesses fail in their first year of operation. The number is much lower for franchise businesses.*

- *If you are a pioneering, visionary person, a franchise business may not be right for you, unless you want to become a franchisor (like Ray Kroc was with McDonald's).*

- *If you buy a franchise business, you will really be in the management business. Your biggest challenge will be hiring and training the right people to run the show. The good news is most franchisors do a good job of preparing you for this.*

Besides franchising, you may also want to look at licensing and, believe it or not, some multi-level businesses (the legal ones). Why? Because your initial investment may be considerably less, and you may have more freedom and flexibility than in a franchise system.

95 Is it easy to start an Internet business?

You can do it. Here are five things you'll need to do it right. Each one starts with a "**D**." You need a:

Distinctive product or service.

Domain name that reflects that brand.

Delivery system where your customers can order and receive your product or service.

Descriptive website. Important: You don't need a lot of "flash"; you need to show the visitor what you can do for them. Usually, the more you tell…the more you sell.

Detailed operational system. Even though your business is online, you still must handle most of the things an old-fashioned business has to deal with, e.g., paying vendors, shipping, returns.

Think of your website as an online brochure. It's very important that you make it clear to browsers how you can help them right now.

96 How can I grow the business I already own?

There are hundreds of ways to do it. However, foundationally speaking the core is found in your determination of what your client service philosophy will be. Always keep this in mind; the way that you build your business grows out of your conviction of what separates you from the rest in your product and in your service. Practically speaking, here are three main thoughts to follow in growing your business. Marketing wizard Jay Abraham's ideas are helpful. You can…

- *Target more customers.*

Understand the value of a customer and determine the value of their patronage. How often do they buy from you? How much do they normally spend? How long do they stay with your business? For example, if your average customer sale is $300, and your typical customer buys three times a year, you earn $900 annually from your average customer. If they stay with you for five years generally, this means that an average customer contributes $4,500 to your gross earnings (over a five-year period). You can see that in this scenario, adding just ten customers would result in a $45,000 increase in sales over five years.

- *Increase the value/price of what you are selling.*

Based on the hypothetical situation I just walked you through, what would happen if you increased your price by just 10%? You might be surprised. If you have 100 customers buying according to the pattern I just described, your annual sales income would go from $90,000 to $100,000. The key to increasing your fees or price is to simultaneously increase the value you are delivering to your customers. Today's customer is more value conscious that ever before. Notice I didn't say price conscious; if customers were more price conscious, we would all be driving Hyundais.

- *Increase the number of purchases your customers make with you.*

Again, with the base of customers I have discussed, now imagine that your customers buy from you four times a year instead of just three. What would that do for your annual income? Well, it would go from $90,000 to $120,000 per year.

Here's where it gets really exciting. If you can increase each of these areas by just a 10% increment, and that is very attainable, your business will grow 30%.

97 What do wealthy people know that I don't?

Not as much as you might imagine. Usually wealthy people, especially those who have earned their way into the money, know a couple of critical things about money. More importantly, they act on them.

If you know about the power of compound interest, act on it.

Put the three main ideas of question 96 into practice!

If you know how to cut your expenses and increase your income, act on them.

Have you ever walked down the aisle of a retail store, noticed some new products, and thought to yourself, "Hey, I had an idea for that!" Well, the main difference between you and the person who got their product on the shelf is not what they knew, it's what they did. They took action. You can, too.

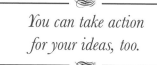

You can take action
for your ideas, too.

What is a financial statement?

These can be drawn up in various ways. One of the best ones is called a "P & L." This simply stands for Profit and Loss statement.

You should learn how to read these and also learn how to create them for your personal and business finances. It's sort of like getting your blood pressure taken. You need to look carefully at:

1. How much money is coming in?

2. How much money is going out?

3. What is the difference between these two?

If your blood pressure is unhealthy, you adjust your diet and exercise. If your money situation is not healthy, you need to make adjustments in your budget, your income, and your necessary expenses.

What is the quickest way to double my money?

Oh, that's easy. Fold it in half and put it back into your pocket!

There is no sure-fire way to quickly double your income. However, if you save and invest the way I have been describing in this book, it is very realistic for you to double your money in a few short years.

Incremental improvements in lowering your expenses, increasing your income, and building your investments, will have a cumulative effect on your finances that is amazing.

And please keep this in mind: When you support God's work

of spreading the Good news about Jesus Christ, your money is more than doubled. It is multiplied in ways you won't even be able to count here on earth.

They need a bigger place for that. It's called Heaven. (John 14:2)

You will feel overwhelmed if you try to make too many changes too soon. Choose the one or two that will give you (and those around you) the biggest lift. COMMIT to those changes and see the difference in your life.

100 How can I spend less than I earn?

Here is an acronym that I think might help you. When it comes to spending **LESS**, try these four ideas:

Lower your wants. And don't confuse your wants with your real needs.

Enlist your family to join you on a debt-reduction and super-savings plan. Make it fun. Make it a game. And see how good it feels to have money to give.

Shop on a full stomach. What this means is you don't want to go to the grocery store when you're hungry. And don't go to the mall and buy clothes just because you are hungry to look cool or get all the latest fashions. Budget before you buy.

Seek out bargains. For example, did you know that you can save on average 15% to 40% by buying generic brands? You can go to a "dress for less" store and often get the same name brands at a fraction of the cost. Make shopping something you do to get what you need, not something you do to fill an emotional need.

By spending less than you earn, you will truly experience how less can be more in your life. You will have more savings, more to give, and more fulfillment in your life this way.

101 What is the bottom line about God and money?

You may have noticed that my answers throughout this book have been based on God's wisdom and not just my experience as a CPA. So, I would like to answer this question by looking at the Biblical Parable of the Talents found in Matthew 25:14-30. In this story three servants are each entrusted with talents of money: One was given five talents, another was given two talents, and the last was given one talent, each according to his ability. The story goes on to tell how the servant with five talents and two talents both doubled their talents by their willingness to take what was entrusted to them and multiply it to please their master; to whom the master replied, "Well done, you have been faithful with a few things, now I will put you in charge of many things." The servant that received one talent went and buried it because he was afraid of losing it. He wasn't willing to give from what had been given to him and the master was very displeased.

As a daily reminder of this parable, I placed in my office lobby three pictures that represent the parable of the talents. All three pictures are of a painter's canvas. The first picture shows one color was given to a painter and the rest of the canvas is only black and white. The second picture shows five colors given to the painter, who multiplied it into ten colors hues making a lovely scene. The last picture shows ten colors given to the painter who multiplied it into twenty color hues that portrayed a wonderful living picture of life. My prayer for you is that this last picture is the color of your life.

Bottom line: Give generously from what God has given to you and God will multiply back more than you can imagine, so that you can give back to Him again and again. Live your life for God, always putting Him first and always giving back abundantly to His kingdom in order to please Him and to do His will. He has proven Himself faithful. He has done it for me. He can do it for you.

———————— ∽ ————————
*Give generously from what
God has given to you.*
———————— ∽ ————————

ABOUT IRS PROBLEM SOLVERS, INC.

"Stop IRS pain and get your life back!"

The only sure thing about IRS problems is that they don't go away by themselves.

If you are suffering from the intense financial pain and psychological pressure that an IRS problem can inflict, IRS Problem Solvers can help.

We care about your problem and can offer you expert solutions. Our specialists represent over 125 years of experience in resolving tax issues including audits, federal tax levies, wage garnishment, liens, and more.

Call 1-877-6-SOLVER or visit
www.YourIRSProblemSolvers.com

ABOUT GOD, MONEY & YOU

"Give more. Make more. Save more."

Put God first. Start giving and start living! Integrate your spiritual and financial life by learning and practicing God-centered principles for your life and your money.

Sign up for our free email newsletter packed with valuable tips, resources, life-changing stories, and more tools for transformation.

www.GodMoneyandYou.com

ABOUT LIBERATORE
ACCOUNTING SERVICES

The firm offers a full range of financial services and solution with a revolutionary approach: "We listen to our clients".

Philip L. Liberatore, Certified Professional Accountant, is a Southern California–based professional corporation providing accounting, consulting, and tax preparation services to businesses and individuals.

The firm offers a full range of financial services and solutions "with a revolutionary approach: We listen to our clients."

For more information, please visit our website:
www.LiberatoreCPA.com

SUGGESTED READING

"Today a reader, tomorrow a leader."
—W. FUSSELMAN

Here are some great books that I recommend for further reading. You'll notice that several of these are old spiritual classics:

- *The Autobiography of George Muller* by George Muller. Read this amazing story and see how God loves to provide for His children and the miracles that take place when you trust Him with all of your needs.

- *Hudson Taylor's Spiritual Secret* by Howard Taylor. This book will knock your socks off about the power of prayer and God's desire to give and bless those that give.

- *Secrets of the Vine* by Bruce Wilkinson. Bruce is a terrific Bible teacher. Don't miss this message about God's abundant love and our need to connect deeply to Him.

- *The Richest Man in Babylon* by George Clason. Before the Automatic Millionaire, before the hundreds of personal finance books, Clason wrote this wonderful fable over 70 years ago. The lessons about earning, saving and debt reduction are still valid today.

- *A Currency of Hope.* This book, published by Debtors Anonymous, offers a proven program for recovery from debt and compulsive spending, based on the 12-steps.

Another important book to purchase is a personal journal. Make notes about your dreams and goals. Keep track of your giving, your earnings, and your savings, and how God is answering your prayers. Watch how God blesses your life and finances when you put Him first!